American Biographies

POCAHONTAS

Gail Fay

Heinemann
LIBRARY

Chicago, Illinois

www.capstonepub.com
Visit our website to find out
more information about
Heinemann-Raintree books.

To order:
☎ Phone 888-454-2279
🖥 Visit www.capstonepub.com
to browse our catalog and order online.

Edited by Abby Colich, Megan Cotugno, and
Laura Hensley
Designed by Cynthia Della-Rovere
Original illustrations © Capstone Global Library
Limited 2011
Illustrated by Oxford Designers & Illustrators
Picture research by Tracy Cummins
Originated by Capstone Global Library Limited
Printed and bound in China by Leo Paper Group

16 15 14 13 12
10 9 8 7 6 5 4 3 2 1

Library of Congress Cataloging-in-Publication Data
Fay, Gail.
 Pocahontas / Gail Fay.
  p. cm.—(American biographies)
 Includes bibliographical references and index.
 ISBN 978-1-4329-6448-1 (hb)—ISBN 978-1-4329-
6459-7 (pb) 1. Pocahontas, d. 1617—Juvenile
literature. 2. Powhatan Indians—Biography—
Juvenile literature. I. Title.
 E99.P85F39 2013
 975.5'01092—dc23   2011037572
 [B]

Acknowledgments
The author and publishers are grateful to the
following for permission to reproduce copyright
material: Alamy: pp. 11 (© North Wind Picture
Archives), 32 (© North Wind Picture Archives);
Corbis: pp. 5 (© W. Langdon Kihn/National
Geographic Society), 37 (© Bettmann); Getty
Images: pp. 17 (Stock Montage), 22 (Universal
History Archive), 29 (MPI), 40 (Joseph Sohm/
Visions of America); Library of Congress Prints and
Photographs Division: pp. 18, 31, 33, 34; North Wind
Picture Archives: pp. 10 (© North Wind), 23 (© North
Wind), 26 (© North Wind); nps.gov: pp. 14, 16, 24,
35 (Sidney E. King), 36; Shutterstock: p. 39 (© Matt
McClain); The Bridgeman Art Library International:
pp. 25 (American School / Private Collection / Peter
Newark Pictures), 28 (Virginia Historical Society,
Richmond, Virginia, USA), 30 (Virginia Historical
Society, Richmond, Virginia, USA); The Granger
Collection, NYC: pp. 7, 20, 21.

Cover photograph of Pocahontas wearing traditional
attire at the time of her marriage to colonialist John
Rolfe, painting by Jean Leon Gerome Ferris, 1754,
reproduced with permission from Getty Images
(Three Lions).

Every effort has been made to contact copyright
holders of material reproduced in this book. Any
omissions will be rectified in subsequent printings if
notice is given to the publisher.

Contents

Some words are shown in bold, **like this**.
These words are explained in the glossary.

Pocahontas, the Playful One

Pocahontas has an important place in U.S. history. She brought food to the starving European settlers who were trying to start a settlement at Jamestown, in present-day Virginia. As a result, the **colonists** survived and Jamestown became the first permanent settlement in North America. Pocahontas was also a peacemaker. She helped keep peace between the English settlers and her people, the Powhatan Indians. She carried messages between her father, Chief Powhatan, and the colonists. Some people say that Pocahontas even rescued one of the colonists from death.

Here is the amazing part: Pocahontas was about 12 years old when these events took place! She was an energetic girl who loved to play with others. Pocahontas and her friends raced along the dirt paths and swam in the rivers. They played games in the open fields. Pocahontas also turned cartwheels with the boys in Jamestown. Today she might have been called a **tomboy**.

Did you know?

When Powhatan children were born, they were given special **tribal** names. The Powhatans believed these names had magical powers to protect them. To save those powers, only family members used a person's tribal name. Everyone else used a nickname. Pocahontas's magical name was Matoaka, but most people called her Pocahontas.

This playful girl also knew when to calm down. She often stood quietly by her father's side as he met with important people. Pocahontas had a special relationship with her father. Colonists later described her as the chief's "dearest daughter."

The name Pocahontas means "mischievous" or "playful." Pocahontas may have been given this nickname because she was so active and curious.

Eyewitness accounts

Most of what people know about Pocahontas comes from the writings of John Smith. Smith and others founded the English **colony** at Jamestown. Smith also became friends with Pocahontas. He wrote five books about the Jamestown settlement.

William Strachey also wrote about Pocahontas. Strachey came to Jamestown in 1610. He wrote about everyday life in Jamestown. He also recorded stories from colonists who had lived in the settlement since it was founded. These stories often involved Pocahontas.

The books by Smith and Strachey are called **primary source** documents. A primary source is something written or created at the time the events occurred. Smith and Strachey wrote about events they witnessed or heard about from others.

Fact VS. Fiction

In one of his primary sources, Smith wrote that Pocahontas saved his life. But did it really happen? Many **historians** say no. Smith is the only person to write about the rescue. He was known to exaggerate, or stretch the truth. Smith told other stories about being saved by beautiful women just like Pocahontas.

Paintings are another type of primary source. John White was an artist who came to North America in 1585. White met Algonquin Indians who shared the same language and lifestyle as Pocahontas and the Powhatans. He saw how these American Indians dressed and what kind of villages they lived in. Then White painted what he saw.

John White painted this watercolor of an Algonquin chief.

Matoaka and the Powhatans

Pocahontas was probably born in 1595 or 1596. Her father named her Matoaka. Pocahontas and the Powhatan Indians are most likely **descendants** of Algonquin Indians who moved from Canada to the eastern Virginia area during the 1300s.

Each Powhatan **tribe** had a **werowance**, or chief. If the chief was a woman, she was called a **weronsqua**. When he was younger, Pocahontas's father **inherited** the position of werowance. He also inherited the name Powhatan, which was the name of the village where he was born. Over the years Chief Powhatan conquered many nearby tribes. These Algonquian-speaking American Indians all became known as Powhatans.

Chief Powhatan

(1540s–1618)

Chief Powhatan was probably born in the 1540s. His birth name was Wahunsonacock. As the highest chief, Powhatan received **tributes**, or gifts, from each of the 30 *werowances* in the **Powhatan Confederacy**. The gifts included pearls, corn, and furs. These tributes made Powhatan rich, and he was able to support many wives. Some **historians** think Powhatan had more than 100 wives! He also had at least 30 children. Chief Powhatan died in 1618.

By the time Pocahontas was born, her father had become the **mamanatowick**, or highest chief, over all the Powhatans. Chief Powhatan ruled over 30 tribes and their *werowances*. He controlled an area that was around 100 miles (160 kilometers) east to west and 100 miles (160 kilometers) north to south. The Powhatans called this area **Tsenacommacah**. The English called it the Powhatan Confederacy.

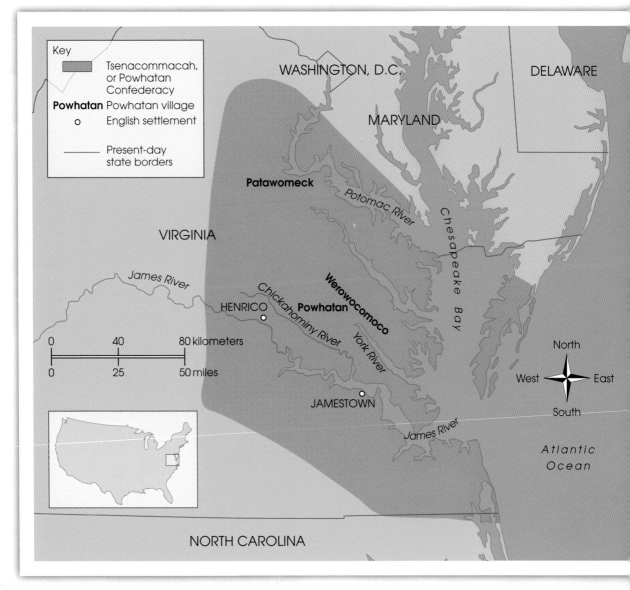

Key

	Tsenacommacah, or Powhatan Confederacy

Powhatan Powhatan village

o English settlement

――― Present-day state borders

WASHINGTON, D.C.

DELAWARE

MARYLAND

Patawomeck

Potomac River

VIRGINIA

Chesapeake Bay

James River

Chickahominy River **Werowocomoco**

HENRICO **Powhatan**

York River

0	40	80 kilometers
0	25	50 miles

North

West — East

South

JAMESTOWN

James River

Atlantic Ocean

NORTH CAROLINA

Life among the Powhatans

Tsenacommacah was located in the **tidewater region** of present-day Virginia. On the east side was Chesapeake Bay. On the west side was the "fall line," where the rivers dropped off into waterfalls. Pocahontas grew up next to one of these rivers in the village of Werowocomoco.

These **waterways** provided a lot of food for the Powhatans. The men made canoes out of hollowed-out trees and fished in the rivers. They also gathered mussels and oysters from Chesapeake Bay. The flat, coastal plain had good soil for farming. The Powhatans grew corn, beans, and squash along the riverbanks.

Powhatan women collected wood, prepared food, and made clothes from animal hides (skins). The women also built houses. They bent thin tree trunks to make the frames and then covered the frames with mats made out of grasses.

Powhatans often protected their villages with tall wooden fences called **palisades**.

Powhatan women broiled fish caught by the men. Powhatans used cooking and eating utensils made from stone, wood, and shells.

Powhatan children, including Pocahontas, played in the woodlands. They probably learned to swim at a young age and knew how to paddle a canoe. The girls learned to make bead necklaces and bracelets. Powhatan children wore little or no clothing until age 12 or 13. William Strachey wrote that young Pocahontas was naked when she turned cartwheels with the boys in Jamestown.

Did you know?

Pocahontas probably played a game that was similar to today's soccer. Players tried to kick a ball through a goal.

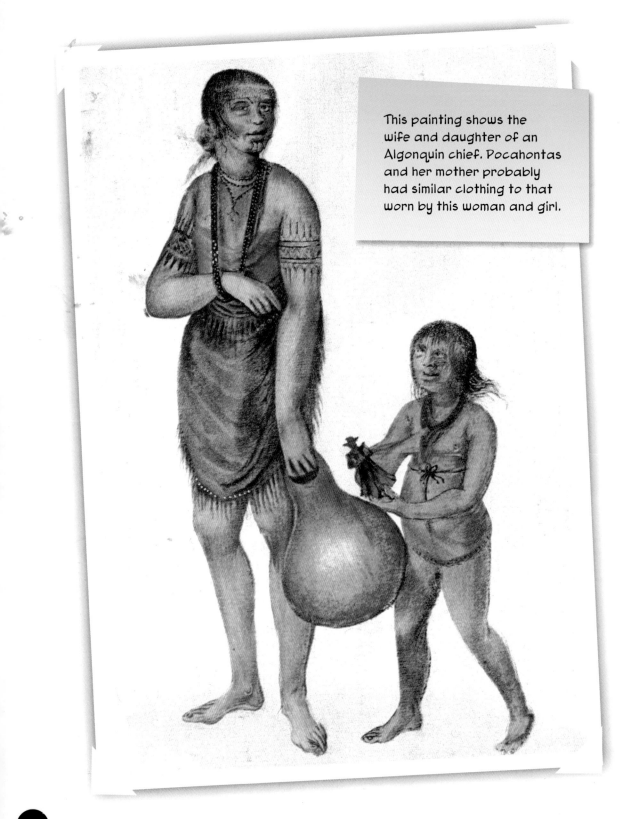

This painting shows the wife and daughter of an Algonquin chief. Pocahontas and her mother probably had similar clothing to that worn by this woman and girl.

Life as a supreme ruler's daughter

Pocahontas was part of a royal family. Her father was the *mamanatowick*, or supreme ruler. As a result, Pocahontas enjoyed many privileges, or advantages. For example, Pocahontas lived in the biggest house in the village. She probably also performed many chores, such as collecting nuts and berries with her friends. She may have also hauled water and carried firewood. She worked in the garden and prepared food.

Pocahontas also learned how to act properly in public. She was probably taught to sit quietly and listen when others were speaking. She may have learned to stand up straight, with her shoulders back. Also, Pocahontas probably received a lot of attention from Chief Powhatan's wives. They likely washed her hair and decorated it with flowers and feathers.

As a daughter of the highest chief, Pocahontas most likely wore jewelry and beads. When she started dressing like a Powhatan woman, her skirts were probably decorated with expensive beads and painted designs.

Did you know?

None of the **primary source** documents mention Pocahontas's mother. This is probably because she was not living in Werowocomoco when the **colonists** arrived. After Pocahontas was born, Chief Powhatan probably sent his wife back to her village. He gave his wife what she needed to raise Pocahontas. At some point, Chief Powhatan brought Pocahontas back to Werowocomoco, and his wife stayed in her village. The chief followed this practice with each of his wives.

13

Friend to the Colonists

When Chief Powhatan went out in public, he often took Pocahontas with him. In April 1607, Pocahontas may have been with her father when he heard that three ships were sailing into Chesapeake Bay.

When the colonists built the Jamestown fort in 1607, it was triangle shaped. This painting shows what Jamestown looked like around 1614.

Did you know?

The **colonists** thought they found a perfect spot for their settlement. However, they soon discovered it was a swampy area with many mosquitoes. Also, the drinking water was very salty and made them sick.

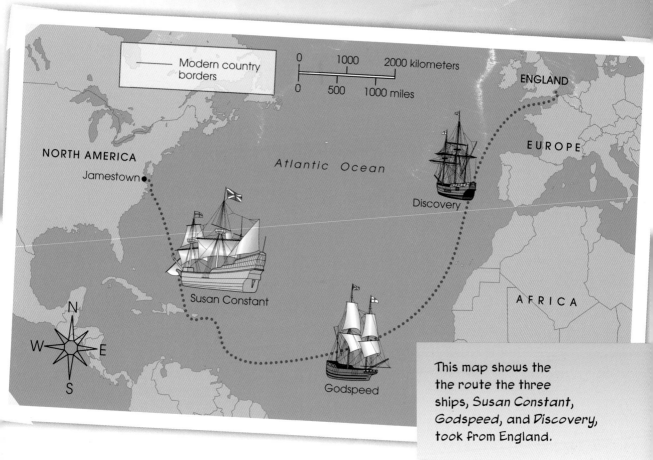

This map shows the the route the three ships, Susan Constant, Godspeed, and Discovery, took from England.

Jamestown is founded

The ships had left England four months earlier. They carried 104 men and no women. The Virginia Company of London paid for the trip. The company wanted to start a **colony** in the Virginia area as a way to make money.

After the ships entered Chesapeake Bay, they sailed up a river. The colonists called it the James River after England's King James I (see page 22). The king had given the Virginia Company permission to start this colony. He hoped the men would find gold in North America.

In May 1607, the Englishmen started building a settlement. They chose a **peninsula**, a piece of land that stuck out into the James River. They built a fort on the peninsula with walls made out of tree trunks. Inside the fort they built simple houses. The colonists named the settlement Jamestown after their king. The settlers did not know they had built their fort on Chief Powhatan's land.

Pocahontas visits Jamestown

The Powhatans had different reactions to the English colonists. Some **tribes** wanted the settlers to leave. They shot arrows at colonists who were out hunting. Other tribes wanted to trade with the colonists. Powhatans traded deer and corn for tools and beads.

The first few months were hard for the colonists. Most were English gentlemen. They did not know how to grow their own food. They were used to having other people do work for them. They were also more interested in finding gold than farming. Because of attacks from American Indians, colonists were afraid to hunt outside the fort. By the end of summer, about half the settlers had died from starvation or disease.

Pocahontas may have taught John Smith Algonquian words to make trading easier.

Chief Powhatan heard about the colonists' troubles. In September he sent Pocahontas and others to Jamestown with corn. **Primary source** documents show that Pocahontas visited Jamestown several times between May and December 1607. She may have met John Smith (see box) during this time. Smith later wrote that Pocahontas saved the colony "from death, famine [starvation], and utter confusion."

Smith became president of the Jamestown colony in September 1608.

John Smith

(about 1580–1631)

Captain John Smith was probably born in 1580. He became a soldier when he was 16. Smith had many adventures in Europe before sailing to North America. He often bragged about what he knew and what he had done. While in North America, Smith explored more than 3,000 miles (4,800 kilometers) of **waterways**. He drew maps of Chesapeake Bay and the surrounding rivers. Smith died in England around age 51.

The rescue legend

In December 1607 Smith set off to find Chief Powhatan. He wanted to trade for more food. During his trip, Smith was kidnapped by Opechancanough, Chief Powhatan's brother. Opechancanough brought Smith to Werowocomoco. Chief Powhatan was waiting for Smith, probably with Pocahontas at his side. They had a feast in Powhatan's **longhouse**.

This image shows Pocahontas saving the life of John Smith.

According to Smith, several Powhatans grabbed him after the meal. They put his head on a stone and were ready to beat him with clubs. Suddenly, Pocahontas threw herself on Smith to protect him. Chief Powhatan stopped the warriors. Then he asked Smith several questions. Why were the English on his land? Did they plan to stay? Smith lied. He told Powhatan that their ship was damaged. They were waiting for another ship to take them back to England. The chief finally let Smith return to Jamestown.

Some **historians** say Powhatan was not really going to kill Smith. He was only testing Smith's courage. Others say Powhatan was performing a ceremony, or ritual, to make Smith an adopted son. Some historians say Smith made it all up. Whatever happened, Smith and Pocahontas became friends after this incident.

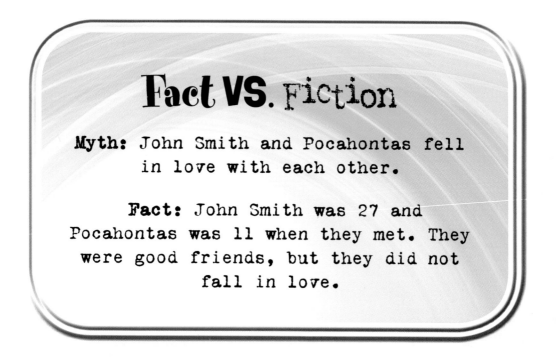

Fact VS. Fiction

Myth: John Smith and Pocahontas fell in love with each other.

Fact: John Smith was 27 and Pocahontas was 11 when they met. They were good friends, but they did not fall in love.

A good relationship ends

In January 1608, a ship arrived from England. It carried food, clothing, and **ammunition**. It also carried 100 settlers. According to some sources, Pocahontas was visiting Jamestown that day. She told her father what she had seen. Chief Powhatan realized Smith had lied to him. The English were not leaving **Tsenacommacah**.

The chief continued trading with the colonists, but he became more demanding. He wanted weapons in exchange for food. When Smith refused, the Powhatans started stealing swords from Jamestown. In response Smith took Powhatan prisoners. Finally, Chief Powhatan told his people to stop trading with the colonists.

In January 1608, a fire destroyed most of Jamestown. When Chief Powhatan heard about it, he sent Pocahontas and others to Jamestown with food for the colonists.

At the same time, Jamestown was running out of food. Many colonists still refused to farm. As president, Smith ordered people to start working. He said, "He that will not work, shall not eat." In January 1609, Smith went to Powhatan and asked for more corn. Powhatan said no. Instead he decided he was tired of having Smith and the colonists on his land. The chief ordered several attacks on Jamestown.

Later, in 1609, Smith was badly injured. When he recovered, he found the colonists no longer wanted him as their president. They thought he was too hard on them. In October 1609, Smith returned to England. He did not say good-bye to his friend Pocahontas. Pocahontas later heard that Smith had died.

Chief Powhatan came up with a plan to kill Smith. Pocahontas found out and warned her friend.

The Missing Years

After Smith returned to England, Pocahontas stopped visiting Jamestown. Perhaps she did not want to go now that her friend was gone. Or perhaps Chief Powhatan ordered her to stop going. Whatever the reason, Pocahontas had little contact with the **colonists** over the next three years. As a result, she does not appear in most of the colonists' writings. **Historians** know little about her life during this time.

In 1609 King James I agreed to let the Jamestown colony continue even though it was not making money.

King James I
(1566–1625)

King James I was born in 1566. He became king of England in 1603. Three years later, King James gave the Virginia Company permission to start a **colony** in Virginia. In 1611 the king authorized, or approved, an English translation of the Bible that is now known as the King James Version. King James died in 1625.

Historians do know that Pocahontas probably married a man named Kocoum in 1610. Pocahontas would have been 14 or 15 years old. Powhatan girls often married at this age. Kocoum was probably a Patawomeck leader. The Patawomeck people were a large **tribe** that belonged to the **Powhatan Confederacy**. Pocahontas probably lived with Kocoum and the Patawomeck from 1610 to 1613.

After Smith left, Chief Powhatan increased his attacks on Jamestown. Powhatan warriors stole weapons from the fort. Colonists set fire to Powhatan villages. Both sides took prisoners. Fighting between Powhatans and colonists continued off and on until 1614. Some historians call this period the First Anglo-Powhatan War.

This is the Virginia Company of London's seal, or official stamp.

The Starving Time

The winter from 1609 to 1610 was extremely cold. The colonists had little food, and they did not get help from Pocahontas or the Powhatans. They could not hunt because they were attacked by Powhatans every time they left the fort. The settlers started eating farm animals, pets, and rats. But it was not enough. Many colonists died that winter. In six months the population of Jamestown went from about 220 to 60. This period is known as the Starving Time because so many people starved to death.

During the Starving Time, colonists dug graves outside the fort when it was dark. They did not want the Powhatans to know how many people had died.

New hope for Jamestown

In May 1610 two ships from England arrived at Jamestown. The passengers expected to find a flourishing colony. Instead they found starving people and burned-down houses. The fort's gates were hanging off their hinges. The colony was in ruins.

The leaders decided it was time to go back to England. As the ships were about to set sail, the passengers saw three English ships heading toward them. The ships carried about 150 settlers, as well as food and supplies. One of the ships also carried Thomas De La Warr, the new governor of Jamestown. He told the ships' captains to turn around. Under De La Warr's direction, the colonists started to rebuild the Jamestown colony.

Delaware Bay, the Delaware River, and the state of Delaware are all named after Thomas De La Warr.

Kidnapped and Baptized

In 1611 Governor De La Warr became sick and returned to England. Sir Thomas Dale took charge of Jamestown until the new governor arrived. Dale was a strict ruler. He forced people to work and punished anyone who broke the rules. He also founded a new settlement northwest of Jamestown. He called it Henrico after King James I's son, Prince Henry.

Captain Argall tricked Pocahontas into visiting his ship. Then he would not let her leave.

Pocahontas becomes a prisoner

In 1612 Sir Thomas Gates became the **colony's** new governor. About 300 people came from England with him. Now there were about 700 people in Jamestown. The **colonists** could not grow enough food to feed everyone.

Most Powhatan **tribes** still refused to trade with the colonists. The Patawomeck people were an exception. They were part of the **Powhatan Confederacy**, but they lived far from Chief Powhatan's village. The Patawomeck *werowance* made many decisions on his own, and he decided to trade with the colonists.

In spring 1612, Captain Samuel Argall sailed up the Potomac River to trade with the Patawomeck people. He discovered that Pocahontas was living there. She was 16 or 17 years old and was no longer with her husband.

A year later, Captain Argall returned to the Patawomeck people. He kidnapped Pocahontas and took her to Jamestown. He told Chief Powhatan that Pocahontas would be freed if the chief sent food and returned stolen weapons. Powhatan did not return the weapons, so Argall kept Pocahontas captive.

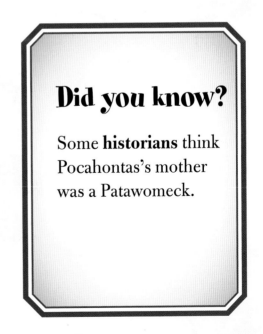

Did you know?

Some **historians** think Pocahontas's mother was a Patawomeck.

Pocahontas becomes Lady Rebecca

Pocahontas did not stay in Jamestown long. The colonists took her to Henrico. This settlement was easier to defend against Powhatans who might try to take Pocahontas back to their chief. In Henrico, Pocahontas stayed with Alexander Whitaker and his family. Whitaker was a young Puritan minister.

This painting shows Pocahontas dressed in the English-style clothing she was forced to wear in Henrico.

As the daughter of the highest Powhatan chief, Pocahontas was considered royalty. The Henrico colonists treated her with kindness and respect. But they also forced Pocahontas to give up her Powhatan **culture**. They wanted her to become a proper English lady. Pocahontas could no longer wear her deerskin skirt. Instead she had to wear an ankle-length skirt and long-sleeved top. She also gave up her **moccasins** and wore English-style shoes.

More importantly, the colonists wanted Pocahontas to become a Christian. They believed **Christianity** was the only true religion. They taught Pocahontas the Lord's Prayer and the Ten Commandments. Pocahontas learned to read English, and she studied the Bible.

Pocahontas was **baptized** in the spring of 1614. She received the Christian name Rebecca. Among the English she was no longer known as Pocahontas.

This painting shows Pocahontas's baptism. Reverend Whitaker performed the ceremony. Some members of Pocahontas's family came to watch.

The Peace of Pocahontas begins

One of Pocahontas's teachers was John Rolfe (see box). He probably met Pocahontas at Reverend Whitaker's church. Rolfe helped Pocahontas learn English and probably read the Bible to her. During this time, Rolfe also fell in love with Pocahontas. He decided that he wanted to marry her.

Rolfe told Thomas Dale about his feelings. In the 1600s, it was not proper for English men to marry American Indian women. Dale approved because he saw the marriage as a sign of peace. He hoped it would end the fighting with the Powhatans.

Rolfe sent a message to Chief Powhatan saying that he wanted to marry Pocahontas. To Rolfe's surprise, the chief approved. Chief Powhatan also agreed to end his war against the colonists. He was nearly 80 years old, and he was tired of fighting.

John Rolfe was about 28 and Pocahontas was about 19 when they got married.

John Rolfe and Pocahontas got married on April 5, 1614. Their marriage marked the beginning of a period the colonists called the Peace of Pocahontas. There was very little fighting between the English and Powhatans for the next eight years.

In 1615 Pocahontas gave birth to a son. The Rolfes named him Thomas.

This illustration shows the wedding of Pocahontas to John Rolfe.

John Rolfe

(about 1585-1622)

John Rolfe was born in England around 1585. He was a hardworking, religious man. Rolfe's first wife died soon after their arrival in North America. In 1612 Rolfe started growing tobacco as a **cash crop**. He experimented with different kinds of seeds and soil until he produced a high-quality tobacco. Rolfe died in 1622.

Lady Rebecca in England

During the Peace of Pocahontas, the **colony** started growing. The leaders needed money to build a school in Henrico. Thomas Dale decided to go to England to find new **investors** who would give money. In 1616 Dale took Pocahontas and her family with him. He hoped people would become interested in the colony after meeting Pocahontas.

In London, Pocahontas went to many parties and met many people. Everywhere Pocahontas went, people took notice. She was dressed well. She spoke English very well. People called Pocahontas a true "Indian princess."

After several weeks Pocahontas started having trouble breathing. The Rolfes moved to a small town outside London, where the air was less damp.

The Rolfes named their son Thomas, probably after Sir Thomas Dale.

Then Pocahontas had a surprise visitor—John Smith. Pocahontas had not seen Smith in eight years. She had thought he was dead! Pocahontas was very upset. She ran out of the room. When she finally returned, they talked for a while, and then Smith left. They never saw each other again.

Did you know?

About 12 Powhatans joined the Rolfes in England. One of them was Tomocomo. Chief Powhatan sent Tomocomo to gather information. What was England like? How many people lived there? Tomocomo was supposed to put a notch in a stick for every person he saw. He soon gave up because there were so many people.

In England, Pocahontas met King James I and Queen Anne. Through a letter from John Smith, the queen learned that Pocahontas had helped the Jamestown colony survive.

The Peacemaker dies

Pocahontas's health did not improve. **Historians** think she had **tuberculosis**, which is a disease that affects the lungs. Tuberculosis was common in England at that time. Pocahontas's son also became sick.

Rolfe and Pocahontas left England in March 1617. They had to leave Thomas with Rolfe's family. He was too sick to travel. The captain sailed down the River Thames toward the Atlantic Ocean. However, he had to stop in Gravesend because Pocahontas was getting worse. Rolfe took his wife to an inn and sent for a doctor.

By the time the doctor arrived, Pocahontas had already died. She was only 21 or 22 years old. Rolfe buried his wife at St. George's Church in Gravesend.

Simon van de Passe made this engraving of Pocahontas while she was in England. It is the only known portrait made during her lifetime.

Tobacco was called "green gold" because it made so much money for the colony.

Shortly after the funeral, Rolfe returned to Virginia without his wife or son. He focused on tobacco farming, which was now making a lot of money. The colony's **economy**, or way of making money, now revolved around **exporting** high-quality tobacco.

Fact VS. Fiction

What did Pocahontas really look like? In many pictures you will see of Pocahontas, it appears she had light skin and a thin face. In reality Pocahontas probably looked like the Powhatan people you have seen in other drawings in this book. She probably had a round face and tan or dark brown skin. Like many Powhatan women, Pocahontas probably had tattoos on her face and body.

The Peace of Pocahontas ends

In Virginia, Rolfe sent word to Chief Powhatan that Pocahontas had died. The chief had moved north to live among the Patawomeck. He had also given up his position as **mamanatowick**. Powhatan's brothers Opitchapan and Opechancanough (see box) were now in charge of the **Powhatan Confederacy**. In April 1618, Chief Powhatan died. He was about 80 years old.

Opechancanough had never liked the **colonists**. Now they were starting new settlements and taking a lot of land to grow tobacco. Opechancanough wanted to reclaim the Powhatans' territory. After Chief Powhatan died, Opechancanough started planning a surprise attack on the colony.

On March 22, 1622, the Peace of Pocahontas suddenly ended. Opechancanough and his warriors attacked several English settlements without any warning. Within an hour, they killed around 350 colonists.

Opechancanough did not attack Jamestown itself. The colonists there had been warned by a young Powhatan boy.

The colonists responded by killing and capturing many Powhatans. They burned Powhatan villages and destroyed their crops. Fighting between Powhatans and colonists continued for 10 years. Some historians refer to this period as the Second Anglo-Powhatan War. It marked the beginning of the end of the Powhatan Confederacy.

taketh the

This engraving shows Opechancanough being threatened by John Smith in 1609.

Chief Opechancanough

(about 1545–about 1646)

Opechancanough was Pocahontas's uncle and Powhatan's younger brother. Opechancanough was the **werowance** of the Pamunkeys, one of the most powerful **tribes** in the Powhatan Confederacy. He later became the *mamanatowick* over all the Powhatans. In 1644 he was captured by the English and later killed. Opechancanough was about 100 years old when he died.

The Peacemaker Lives On

Without help from Pocahontas, the Jamestown settlement would have probably collapsed soon after it started. She provided food. She warned Smith and others of danger. As a result, Jamestown survived. It became the first permanent settlement in North America. In 1619 Jamestown became the capital of the Virginia **colony**.

Opechancanough's attempt to destroy the colony in 1622 did not work. In fact, the **colonists** took even more Powhatan land. Opechancanough tried another surprise attack in 1644. He killed over 300 colonists, but the colony did not collapse.

In 1635 Pocahontas's son, Thomas, returned to Virginia. He was 20 years old. His father and grandfather had already died. When Thomas arrived, he found that his grandfather, Chief Powhatan, had given him a lot of land. Thomas became a tobacco farmer like his father.

Did you know?

Several English words used today come from the Virginia Algonquian language spoken by Pocahontas and her people. Here are some examples:

• hominy: corn; from *uskatahomen*

• **moccasin**: shoe; from *mockasin*

• raccoon: animal that comes out at night; from *raugroughcun*

• tomahawk: ax used as a missile or weapon; from *tomahack*

In 1699 the capital of the Virginia colony was moved from Jamestown to Middle Plantation, which was later named Williamsburg. After this, Jamestown started falling apart. By the mid-1700s, the settlement at Jamestown was gone, but its historic importance lives on.

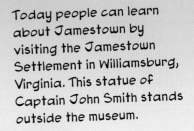

Today people can learn about Jamestown by visiting the Jamestown Settlement in Williamsburg, Virginia. This statue of Captain John Smith stands outside the museum.

CAPTAIN
JOHN SMITH
GOVERNOR OF
VIRGINIA
1608

This statue of Pocahontas stands at the Jamestown Settlement in Virginia. There is a similar statue at the church in Gravesend, England, where Pocahontas is buried.

The Powhatans today

Pocahontas is remembered as a peacemaker. As a child, she was sent to Jamestown with food as a sign of peace. As an adult, Pocahontas brought peace through her marriage to John Rolfe.

The Peacemaker's death was followed by years of fighting. Many colonists and Powhatans died. The English finally won. They forced the Powhatans to leave parts of **Tsenacommacah** and move onto small **reservations**. The Powhatans could not build houses or hunt outside these reservations. Powhatans had to change their way of life since these reservations were sometimes far from the **waterways** that provided food.

Over the years, the Powhatan population decreased due to disease, starvation, and fighting. When Pocahontas was born in 1595 or 1596, around 14,000 Powhatans lived in the **tidewater region** of Virginia. By 1669 that number had dropped to 1,800.

But Pocahontas's people have not completely disappeared. Thousands of Powhatans still live in Virginia and other parts of the United States. Two Powhatan **tribes** still control the reservations that were established in the 1600s. They are the Pamunkeys and the Mattaponis. Since the early 1980s, other Powhatan tribes have reorganized themselves. In all, eight Powhatan tribes are officially recognized in Virginia today.

Did you know?

There are people alive today who are directly related to Pocahontas. They are **descendants** of Pocahontas's son, Thomas, and his wife, Jane Poythress.

Timeline

1300s
Algonquian-speaking American Indians from Canada move to the tidewater region of present-day Virginia.

1540s
Chief Powhatan is born as Wahunsonacock.

1595 or 1596
Pocahontas is born as Matoaka.

November 1606
King James I gives the Virginia Company of London permission to form a colony in the tidewater region of modern-day Virginia.

January 1608
Fire destroys most of Jamestown.

December 1607
John Smith is kidnapped by Opechancanough and taken to Werowocomoco. He later writes of being rescued by Pocahontas.

May 1607
English settlers start building the Jamestown colony. Pocahontas starts visiting Jamestown shortly afterward.

April 1607
The ships *Susan Constant*, *Godspeed*, and *Discovery* enter Chesapeake Bay.

October 1609
John Smith returns to England.

Winter 1609-1610
This period is known as the Starving Time.

1610
Pocahontas marries Kocoum and moves to a Patawomeck village.

1610
Settlers decide to leave Jamestown, but Sir Thomas De La Warr orders the ships back to shore, and the colony is rebuilt.

April 1614
Pocahontas marries John Rolfe. The Peace of Pocahontas begins.

Spring 1614
Pocahontas is baptized and named Rebecca.

Spring 1613
Captain Samuel Argall kidnaps Pocahontas.

1612
John Rolfe starts growing tobacco in Jamestown.

1611
Sir Thomas Dale founds the Henrico settlement.

January 1615
Pocahontas's son, Thomas, is born.

Spring 1616
Pocahontas and her family go with Sir Thomas Dale to England.

March 1617
Pocahontas dies in Gravesend, England. John Rolfe returns to Jamestown.

1618
Chief Powhatan dies. Opechancanough and his brother become rulers of the Powhatan Confederacy.

1646
The English start forcing Powhatans onto reservations.

1644
Opechancanough is kidnapped and later killed.

1622
Opechancanough launches a surprise attack on English settlements, and the Peace of Pocahontas ends.

1622
John Rolfe dies.

Family Tree

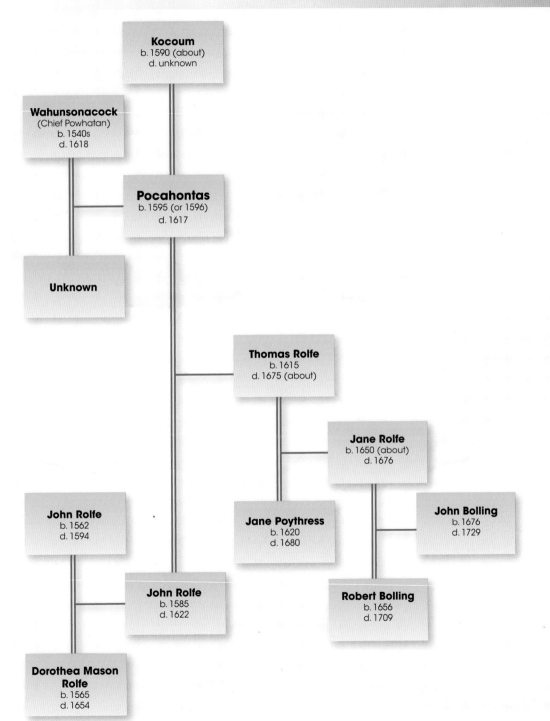

Kocoum
b. 1590 (about)
d. unknown

Wahunsonacock
(Chief Powhatan)
b. 1540s
d. 1618

Pocahontas
b. 1595 (or 1596)
d. 1617

Unknown

Thomas Rolfe
b. 1615
d. 1675 (about)

Jane Rolfe
b. 1650 (about)
d. 1676

John Rolfe
b. 1562
d. 1594

Jane Poythress
b. 1620
d. 1680

John Bolling
b. 1676
d. 1729

John Rolfe
b. 1585
d. 1622

Robert Bolling
b. 1656
d. 1709

Dorothea Mason Rolfe
b. 1565
d. 1654

Glossary

ammunition
material, such as bullets, fired from a weapon

baptize
to ceremonially make someone a part of the Christian church

cash crop
crop grown for the purpose of selling it

Christianity
religion based on the life and beliefs of Jesus Christ

colonist
person who lives in a colony

colony
distant territory belonging to a nation

culture
shared beliefs, traditions, and behaviors belonging to a certain group of people

descendant
offspring, or relative, who is directly related to previous family members

economy
way a nation or state uses its resources to make money

export
to ship crops or products to another country

historian
person who studies history

inherit
to receive money, property, or a position through the family line

investor
someone who puts money into a project or account with the hope of earning more money

longhouse
type of long, narrow house used by American Indians

mamanatowick
Algonquian word for the highest-ranking chief of the Powhatan Confederacy

mischievous
enjoying having fun and causing a bit of trouble

moccasin
leather shoe worn by various American Indian tribes

palisade
fence of tall wood stakes

peninsula
piece of land that is almost entirely surrounded by water

Powhatan Confederacy
group of Algonquian-speaking American Indian tribes in modern-day Virginia; the land area where those tribes lived

primary source
something written or created at the time the events took place

reservation
area of land set aside for and controlled by an American Indian tribe

tidewater region
area in eastern Virginia near Chesapeake Bay; also called the coastal plain

tomboy
girl who likes to take part in physical activities and play sports

tribal
having to do with a tribe

tribe
group that shares a common purpose, language, and culture

tribute
gift given as a sign of respect

Tsenacommacah
Algonquian word for the homeland of the Algonquian-speaking American Indian tribes in eastern Virginia

tuberculosis
serious disease that affects the lungs and other parts of the body and that can be passed on to others

waterway
body of water such as a river or bay

weronsqua
Algonquian word for female tribal chief or leader

werowance
Algonquian word for male tribal chief or leader

Find Out More

Books

Brimner, Larry Dane. *Pocahontas: Bridging Two Worlds.* Tarrytown, N.Y.: Marshall Cavendish, 2008.

Harkins, Susan Sales, and William H. Harkins. *What's So Great About Pocahontas?* Hockessin, Del.: Mitchell Lane, 2008.

Jenner, Caryn. *Pocahontas.* New York: Dorling Kindersley, 2009.

Jones, Victoria Garrett. *Pocahontas: A Life in Two Worlds.* New York: Sterling, 2010.

Sita, Lisa. *Pocahontas: The Powhatan Culture and the Jamestown Colony.* New York: PowerPlus Books, 2005.

DVDs

Biography: Pocahontas—Ambassador of the New World. A&E Home Video, 2005.

Pocahontas Revealed. WGBH Boston, 2007.

Websites

Jamestown Settlement and Yorktown Victory Center
www.historyisfun.org/
This is the website of the Jamestown Settlement in Williamsburg, Virginia. It has information about the museums and the outdoor living history displays at the Jamestown Settlement. It also has links to short articles, videos, and podcasts about Pocahontas, Jamestown, the Powhatan Indians, and more.

The Real Pocahontas
http://pocahontas.morenus.org/
This website has information on Pocahontas, Chief Powhatan, John Smith, and more. It includes two charts comparing the real story of Pocahontas with the Disney movies *Pocahontas* and *Pocahontas II*. This website also has a family tree of Pocahontas's descendants, as well as a list of books on Pocahontas and Jamestown.

Powhatan Indian Fact Sheet
www.bigorrin.org/powhatan_kids.htm
This website has information on the Powhatan Indians who lived in Virginia. Topics include Powhatan houses, clothing, religion, food, and more.

Powhatan Museum of Indigenous Arts and Culture
www.powhatanmuseum.com/
This website has links to information on Pocahontas, Chief Powhatan, Powhatan's brother Opechancanough, the Powhatan Indians today, and more. It includes a map showing the area controlled by Powhatan. It also has a Children's Corner link where you can learn which English words of today come from the Algonquian language.

Places to visit

Jamestown Settlement
2110 Jamestown Road
Williamsburg, VA 23185
888-593-4682
www.historyisfun.org/jamestown-settlement.htm

Pamunkey Indian Tribe Museum
175 Lay Landing Road
King William, VA 23086
804-843-4792
www.pamunkey.net/museum.html

Smithsonian National Museum of the American Indian
Fourth Street & Independence Avenue, SW
Washington, DC 20560
202-633-1000
www.nmai.si.edu/

Index